Anonymus

Catalogue of the Architectural Exhibition

Anonymus

Catalogue of the Architectural Exhibition

ISBN/EAN: 9783742833891

Manufactured in Europe, USA, Canada, Australia, Japa

Cover: Foto ©Thomas Meinert / pixelio.de

Manufactured and distributed by brebook publishing software
(www.brebook.com)

Anonymus

Catalogue of the Architectural Exhibition

BOSTON ARCHITECTURAL EXHIBITION

ILLUSTRATED CATALOGUE

OCTOBER, 1891

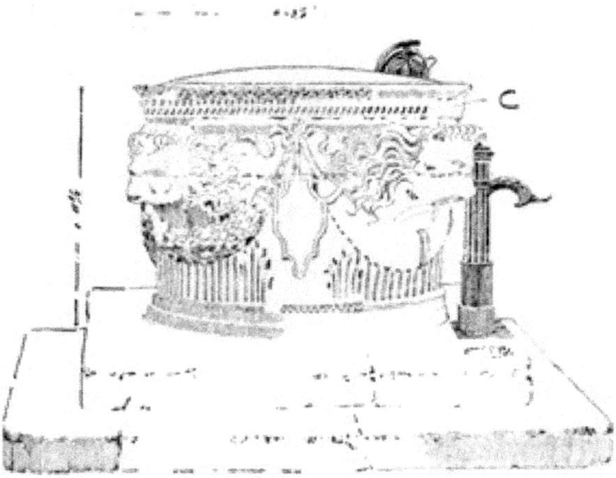

WELL-CURB, VENICE. DRAWN BY A. KAHN.

OF THE ARCHITECTURAL EXHIBITION HELD IN THE NEW PUBLIC LIBRARY BUILDING, OCTOBER 28 TO NOVEMBER 4, INCLUSIVE, IN CONJUNCTION WITH THE ANNUAL CONVENTION OF THE AMERICAN INSTITUTE OF ARCHITECTS, AND UNDER THE DIRECTION

OF THE

BOSTON SOCIETY OF ARCHITECTS

AND THE

BOSTON ARCHITECTURAL CLUB

BOSTON, MASS.
1891

Committees on the Exhibition

General Committees

From the Society of Architects

John A. Fox — A. W. Longfellow — E. M. Wheelwright
C. H. Blackall — A. G. Everett — R. C. Sturgis

From the Boston Architectural Club

C. H. Blackall — A. G. Everett — R. C. Sturgis — W. C. Norris

Executive Committee

C. H. Blackall — W. C. Norris

Committee on Reception and Awards

E. C. Cabot — C. A. Cummings — C. H. Walker
E. M. Wheelwright

DRAWN BY T. RAFFLES DAVISON.

Boston Society of Architects

President

EDWARD C. CABOT

Vice-President

CHAS. A. CUMMINGS

Treasurer

WILLIAM G. PRESTON

Secretary

H. LANGFORD WARREN

Fellows.

Francis R. Allen, 220 Devonshire Street.
J. M. Allen, Marion, Mass.
Robert D. Andrews, 8 Beacon Street.
W. D. Austin, 6 Beacon Street.
C. H. Blackall, Music Hall Building.
Charles Brigham, 22 Beacon Street.
J. M. Brown, 68 Devonshire Street.
Edward C. Cabot, High Street, Brookline.
William E. Chamberlin, 293 Harvard Street, Cambridgeport.
Frank W. Chandler, Institute of Technology.
Theodore M. Clark, 22 Congress Street.
Charles A. Cummings, 230 Clarendon Street.
Charles A. Coolidge, 13 Exchange Street.
William H. Dabney, 9 Park Street.
Stephen C. Earle, Worcester, Mass.
W. Ralph Emerson, 85 Water Street.
Arthur G. Everett, 60 Devonshire Street.
Carl Fehmer, 87 Milk Street.
John A. Fox, Phillips Building.
E. C. Gardner, Springfield, Mass.
George F. Hammond, Cleveland, O.
Alfred B. Harlow, 6 Beacon Street.
Henry W. Hartwell, 68 Devonshire Street.
Henry S. Hunnewell, 9 Park Street.
Herbert Jaques, 8 Beacon Street.
James T. Kelley, 57 Mt. Vernon Street.
W. Whitney Lewis, 85 Water Street.
Edwin J. Lewis, Jr., 9 Park Street.
Arthur Little, Mason Building.
Alexander W. Longfellow, Jr., 6 Beacon Street.
W. P. P. Longfellow, 18 Huntington Avenue.
George F. Loring, 10 Tremont Street.
Charles F. McKim, 57 Broadway, New York City.
S. W. Mead, 60 Devonshire Street.
Robert S. Peabody, Exchange Building.
Sanford Phipps, 10 Tremont Street.
William G. Preston, 186 Devonshire Street.
J. Pickering Putnam, 4 Pemberton Square.
Joseph R. Richards, 44 Court Street.
William P. Richards, 44 Court Street.
William C. Richardson, 68 Devonshire Street.
Warren A. Rodman, 54 Devonshire Street.
Arthur Rotch, 85 Devonshire Street.
J. A. Schweinfurth, 60 Devonshire Street.
Willard T. Sears, Mason Building.
George R. Shaw, 9 Park Street.

George Snell, Studio Building.
John G. Stearns, Exchange Building.
F. W. Stickney, 131 Devonshire Street.
George F. Shepley, 13 Exchange Street.
R. Clipston Sturgis, 19 Exchange Place.
George T. Tilden, 85 Devonshire Street.
Henry Vaughan, 5 Pemberton Square.
C. Howard Walker, 6 Beacon Street.
William R. Ware, 211 Tremont Street.
H. Langford Warren, 9 Park Street.
George H. Wetherell, 3 Hamilton Place.
Edmund M. Wheelwright, 6 Beacon Street.
William M. Whidden, Portland, Oregon.
Walter T. Winslow, 3 Hamilton Place.
Franz E. Zerrahn, 9 Hamilton Place.

Junior Members.

Albert C. Fernald, 78 Devonshire Street.
A. S. Jenney, 53 Beacon Street.
George F. Newton, 60 Devonshire Street.
Henry A. Phillips, Exchange Building, Boston.
George F. Rivinius, Northfield, Mass.
Jaque Van Straaten, 19 Exchange Place.

Honorary Members.

Francis H. Bacon, 96 Washington Street.
J. Thacher Clark, Harrow, England.
William D. Howells, 184 Commonwealth Avenue.
Charles H. Moore, Cambridge.
Edward S. Morse, Salem, Mass.
Charles E. Norton, Cambridge, Mass.
F. L. Olmstead, Brookline, Mass.
Augustus St. Gaudens, 57 Broadway, New York City.
William R. Ware, Columbia College, New York City.

Associate Members.

Ernest W. Bowditch, 60 Devonshire Street.
R. Brown, Jr., 96 Washington Street.
James Brough, 8 Bosworth Street.
George R. Clark, 48 Boylston Street.
Charles Eliot, 50 State Street.
John C. Olmstead, Brookline.
D. W. Ross, Cambridge, Mass.
H. B. Warren, Hillside Avenue, Roxbury.
S. D. Warren, Jr., 220 Devonshire Street.

BOSTON ARCHITECTURAL CLUB

President

C. H. BLACKALL

Treasurer

JOSEPH E. CHANDLER

Secretary

H. D. HALE

Directory

To serve until October, 1892

GEO. H. WETHERELL JOSEPH E. CHANDLER
C. H. BLACKALL G. F. NEWTON
H. D. HALE

To serve until October, 1893

E. F. MAHER H. L. WARREN

Steward

JAMES A. MORRIS

List of Members

PROFESSIONALS

Willard P. Adden
Chas. H. Alden
Will S. Aldrich
Francis R. Allen
R. D. Andrews
Walter Atherton
H. B. Ball
Geo. A. Ballantine
Edw. T. Barker
Geo. E. Barton
John W. Bemis
E. R. Benton
H. F. Bigelow
C. W. Bixby
C. H. Blackall
Dwight Blaney
Allan E. Boone
W. W. Bosworth
A. H. Bowditch
Samuel J. Brown
H. W. C. Browne
A. C. Bubier
Edward C. Cabot
W. R. Cabot
F. W. Chandler
Jos. E. Chandler
J. H. Chapman
W. C. Chase
Eugene L. Clark
W. J. Clark
Albert W. Cobb
Ogden Codman, Jr.
Robert Coit
Chas. A. Coolidge
Frank Irving Cooper
J. M. Corner
Ralph Adams Cram
G. W. Crockett
C. F. Crosby
Edw. Percy Dana
Alfred L. Darrow
G. R. Dean
R. N. Dow
Stephen A. Drew
Jas. Driver
W. N. Dudley
Chas. B. Dunham
Ernest H. Elliot
A. G. Everett
John L. Faxon
Frank W. Ferguson
Geo. P. Fernald
Lyman A. Ford
J. Chandler Fowler
J. Sumner Fowler
H. S. Frazer
Jos. B. Gay
Robt. W. Gibbon
D. P. Goodrich
D. C. Hale

John J. Haley
John W. Hall
Geo. C. Harding
H. C. Hayward
Augustus B. Higginson
C. M. Hill
H. C. Holt
Richard Hooker
John G. Howard
Wallis E. Howe
Edward H. Hoyt
Franklin H. Hutchins
Herbert Jaques
Barton P. Jenks
I. H. Jones
Jas. F. Kavanaugh
Jas. T. Kelley
Wm. G. Kerr
Walter H. Kilham
J. A. Lane
J. S. Lee
Arthur Little
Chas. A. Little
R. K. Longfellow
John A. Mack
Charles D. Maginnis
E. F. Maher
J. R. Mann
J. L. Mauran
C. Herbert McClare
Clarence F. McFarland
H. S. McKay
Wm. H. McLean
Henry A. Mears
P. B. Metcalf
Junius H. Morse
E. A. P. Newcomb
Geo. F. Newton
Geo. Leslie Nichols
W. H. Nichols
W. W. Northend
H. W. Northey
E. P. Overmire
Clarence F. Palmer
Herman Parker
Charles E. Patch
R. S. Peabody
Austin W. Pease
W. Y. Peters
H. T. Pratt
W. G. Preston
Geo. J. Porter
A. W. Rice
Walter E. Rice
W. C. Richardson
H. G. Ripley
Edward Little Rogers
F. A. Schiller
W. T. Sears
L. A. Simon
Frank W. Smith
E. E. Soderholtz
R. C. Spencer, Jr.
Arthur C. Sprague
H. M. Stephenson
Edward F. Stevens
Geo. W. Stone
R. C. Sturgis
Matthew Sullivan
Geo. A. Swift
Bertrand Taylor
P. A. Tracey
Alex. Buel Trowbridge
Frank W. Tucker
Chas. R. Tuckett
F. Jos. Untersee
Hugh Vallance
Jacque Van Straaten
F. M. Wakefield
G. C. Wales
C. H. Walker
W. L. Walker
T. F. Walsh
H. L. Warren
R. A. Watson
W. S. Wells

C. F. Wentworth
W. P. Wentworth
Geo. H. Wetherell
Henry W. Wilkinson
E. I. Wilson
W. F. Winslow
A. H. Wright
E. E. Ziegler

NON-PROFESSIONALS

Chas. J. Bacon
Francis H. Bacon
John C. Baird
C. M. Baker
H. D. Bates
Geo. S. Brazer
C. Dudley Brown
Robert Casson
H. E. Clifford
W. G. Corthell
Ervin E. Crook
Geo. DeVere Curtis
A. B. Cutter
Capt. John S. Damrell
A. H. Davenport
E. Eldon Deane
H. E. Doering
Horace C. Dunham
John Evans
Louis C. Flagg
Edwin Ford
Henry F. Gibbs
D. A. Gregg
Wm. H. Grueby
Irving T. Guild
A. Haberstroh
Robert W. Jackson
Harvey L. Jones
Geo. W. Keats
L. E. Kimball
E. R. Kingsbury
I. Kirchmyer
Chas. E. Landerkin
Jas. G. Lincoln
J. Harry Mann
John E. Muldoon
Herbert W. Munn
A. H. Munsell
Wm. C. Norris
Henry B. Pennell
Geo. W. Perkins
Lewis F. Perry
H. J. Phipps
Denman W. Ross
Arthur H. Smith
W. B. Summers
Henry A. Turner
Ross Turner
Ottoman Wallburg
C. F. Whittemore
Harry Wood

HONORARY MEMBERS

Ernest George
H. P. Kirby
J. E. Pennell
Harold A. Peto
Prof. Wm. R. Ware

Catalogue of Drawings

1 DESIGN FOR BUILDING FOR AMERICAN FINE ARTS. By J. A. Schweinfurth.

2 DESIGN FOR LIBRARY IN EMPIRE STYLE. Doe, Hunnewell, & Co.

3 DESIGN FOR DINING-ROOM IN RENAISSANCE. By Doe, Hunnewell, & Co.

4 DESIGN FOR ELIZABETHAN HALL. By Doe, Hunnewell, & Co.

5 DESIGN FOR PARLOR, LOUIS XVI. STYLE. By Doe, Hunnewell, & Co.

6 PRIZE DRAWINGS, MONTHLY COMPETITION, SKETCH CLUB OF NEW YORK. By E. E. Edwards, Al. C. Marsh, Julius Harder.

7 WATER-COLOR STUDIES, WILTON, N.H. By Ross Turner.

8 DESIGN FOR STAINED GLASS WINDOW. By Edward Ford and Frederick Brooks.

9 DESIGN FOR CITY CHURCH. By Bosworth & Chase.

10 MONTHLY COMPETITION, PRIZE DRAWINGS, SKETCH CLUB OF NEW YORK. Chas. H. Israels, F. L. V. Hoppin, B. G. Goodhue, J. Nat Hutchins, F. W. Penn, F. R. Hirsh, Willis K. Polk.

11 MONTHLY COMPETITION, SKETCH CLUB OF NEW YORK. A VILLAGE WELL-HOUSE. Drawn by Chas. H. Darsh.

12 TOWER OF AGNES SOREL, AT LORCHES. Drawn by A. W. Brunner.

13 DESIGN FOR UNITARIAN CHURCH, WALNUT ST., BROOKLINE. Sturgis & Cabot, Architects.

14 MAIN ENTRANCE, TEMPLE BETH EL, N.Y. Brunner & Tryon, Architects.

15 HILLSIDE PRESBYTERIAN CHURCH, ORANGE, N.J. Rossiter & Wright, Architects.

16 STOKESAY CASTLE, SALOP. Drawn by J. H. Cook. R.I.B.A. Silver medal, 1887.

17 TOMB OF LOUIS DE BREZE, ROUEN CATHEDRAL. Etching by Jas. Ackerman.

18 INTERIOR OF MOSQUE. Drawn by Mrs. A. F. Jacossey.

19 THE EMMA S. CLARK MEMORIAL LIBRARY, SETAUKET, L.I. Rossiter & Wright, Architects.

20 COMPETITIVE DESIGN FOR THE MONTREAL BOARD OF TRADE BUILDING. Rotch & Tilden, Architects.

21 EQUITABLE BUILDING, DES MOINES, IA. STUDY FOR MAIN HALL AND STAIRCASE. Andrews, Jaques, & Rantoul, Architects.

22 THE EQUITABLE BUILDING, DENVER, COL. Andrews, Jaques, & Rantoul, Architects.

23 EQUITABLE BUILDING, DES MOINES, IA. Andrews, Jaques, & Rantoul, Architects.

24 HOUSE AT BROOKLINE. Andrews, Jaques, & Rantoul, Architects.

25 HOUSE AT CAMBRIDGE. Andrews, Jaques, & Rantoul, Architects.

26 BOSTON BUILDING, DENVER, COL. Andrews, Jaques, & Rantoul, Architects.

27 HOUSE AT YORK HARBOR. Andrews, Jaques, & Rantoul, Architects.

28 HOUSE AT BROOKLINE. Andrews, Jaques, & Rantoul, Architects.

29 SKETCH FOR HOUSE IN WASHINGTON. Little & Brown, Architects.

30 HOUSE AT SWAMPSCOT. Little, Brown, & Moore, Architects.

31 BALL-ROOM FOR MRS. WIRT DEXTER, CHICAGO. Little, Brown, & Moore, Architects.

32 SUGGESTION FOR REBUILDING THE PEABODY INSTITUTE, DANVERS, MASS. Little, Brown, & Moore, Architects.

33 PROPOSED ALTERATION OF HALL, 59 COMMONWEALTH AVENUE, BOSTON. Little & Brown, Architects.

34 DRAWING-ROOM OF MR. ARTHUR LITTLE, 8 COMMONWEALTH AVENUE.

35 DINING-ROOM OF MRS. G. R. EMMERTON, SALEM. Little, Brown, & Moore, Architects.

36 MUSIC-ROOM FOR MRS. OLE BULL, CAMBRIDGE. Little, Brown, & Moore, Architects.

37 MASTER BUILDERS' EXCHANGE, BOSTON. PLANS AND VIEWS. John A. Fox, Architect.

38 HOUSE FOR A. W. BENTON, NEWTON CENTRE, MASS. E. R. Benton, Architect.

39 STORES AND OFFICES, WINTER AND TREMONT STREETS, BOSTON. John A. Fox, Architect.

40 HOUSE FOR A. F. ADAMS, NEWTON, MASS. John A. Fox, Architect.

41 HOUSE AT CHESTNUT HILL. Chapman & Frazer, Architects.

42 HOUSE AT CHESTNUT HILL, INTERIOR. Chapman & Frazer, Architects.

43 BUSINESS BUILDINGS AT HELENA AND BUTTE CITY, MONT. Paulsen & Lavalle, Architects.

44 THE MONTANA CLUB, HELENA, MONT. Paulsen & Lavalle, Architects.

45 HOUSE AT WOOD'S HOLL, FOR M. OGDEN JONES. Wheelwright & Haven, Architects.

46 BROADWATER NATATORIUM, INTERIOR, HELENA, MONT. Paulsen & Lavalle, Architects.

47 BROADWATER NATATORIUM, EXTERIOR, HELENA, MONT. Paulsen & Lavalle, Architects.

48 HOUSE FOR GEORGE P. HOWLETT. C. Herbert McClare, Architect.

49 HOUSE FOR A. H. OVERMAN, SPRINGFIELD, MASS. E. R. Benton, Architect.

50 MASONIC BUILDING, DOVER, N.H. Hartwell & Richardson, Architects.

51 DESIGN FOR A CITY CHURCH. Hartwell & Richardson, Architects.

52 DESIGN FOR NEWTON CLUB HOUSE. Rotch & Tilden, Architects.

53 DESIGN FOR ROBBINS MEMORIAL LIBRARY, ARLINGTON, MASS. Cabot, Everett, & Mead, Architects.

54 DESIGN FOR OFFICE BUILDING. Rotch & Tilden, Architects.

55 HOUSE FOR THOMAS E. PROCTOR, Esq., COMMONWEALTH AVENUE. Hartwell & Richardson, Architects.

56 SAVINGS BANK BUILDING, DEDHAM, MASS. Hartwell & Richardson, Architects.

57 MAY HALL STATE NORMAL SCHOOL, FRAMINGHAM, MASS. Hartwell & Richardson, Architects.

58 NATIONAL BANK BUILDING, WALTHAM, MASS. Hartwell & Richardson, Architects.

59 FIRST PARISH CONGREGATIONAL CHURCH, WAKEFIELD, MASS. Hartwell & Richardson, Architects.

60 STATE NORMAL SCHOOL, BRIDGEWATER, MASS. Hartwell & Richardson, Architects.

61 SKETCH FOR HOUSE AT NEWTON, MASS. E. J. Lewis, Jr., Architect.

62 SKETCH FOR HOUSE AT ASHMONT. E. J. Lewis, Jr., Architect.

63 WOLLASTON UNITARIAN CHURCH. E. J. Lewis, Jr., Architect.

64 SKETCH FOR HOUSE AT ASHMONT. E. J. Lewis, Jr., Architect.

65 DESIGN FOR A PAVILION FOR STATUE OF ZEUS. Gold medal of the Architectural League, N.Y., 1890. Harold Magonigle.

66 MEMORIAL HALL AND LIBRARY, BROCKTON, MASS. Kendall & Stevens, Architects.

67 RESIDENCE OF E. O. ACHORN, BROOKLINE, MASS. J. A. Schweinfurth, Architect.

68 STUDY FOR A VILLA. J. A. Schweinfurth, Architect.

69 RESIDENCE OF SIDNEY HOMER, ARLINGTON, MASS. J. A. Schweinfurth, Architect.

70 DESIGN FOR BUILDING FOR AMERICAN FINE ARTS SOCIETY, NEW YORK. J. A. Schweinfurth, Architect.

71 DESIGN FOR CEMETERY MONUMENT, AUBURN, N.Y. J. A. Schweinfurth, Architect.

72 DESIGN FOR A RESIDENCE IN BROOKLINE, MASS. J. A. Schweinfurth, Architect.

73 THE GIRALDA TOWER, SEVILLE. Drawn by J. A. Schweinfurth.

74 PORCH OF KING'S COLLEGE, CANTERBURY, ENG. Drawn by Will S. Aldrich.

75 WORCESTER COLLEGE, OXFORD, ENG. Drawn by Will S. Aldrich.

76 ODD FELLOWS' BUILDING, LOWELL, MASS. Merrill & Cutler, Architects. Drawn by H. B. Pennell.

77 STABLE FOR W. F. WELD, BROOKLINE, MASS. Wheelwright & Haven, Architects.

78 THE ZINZENDORF HOTEL, WINSTON, N.C. Wheelwright & Haven, Architects.

79 LIBRARY FOR C. E. ALEXANDER, NEW YORK. By George A. Glaenzer & Jos. H. Taft.

80 THE SCRIPP'S BUILDING, DETROIT. Mason & Rice, Architects.

81 HOUSE FOR PETER E. BAKER, BROOKLINE. Samuel J. Brown, Architect.

82 HOUSE FOR T. B. GRIGGS, BROOKLINE. Samuel J. Brown, Architect.

83 VESTIBULE, ST. MARK'S, VENICE. Drawn by J. Linden Smith.

84 COLONNADE OF DOGE'S PALACE, VENICE. Drawn by J. Linden Smith.

85 FURNITURE DESIGNS. By C. E. Landerkin.

86 VILLAGE CHURCH. John Zettel, Architect.

87 STABLE FOR W. F. WELD, BROOKLINE, MASS. Wheelwright & Haven, Architects.

88 GALLERY OF HENRI II., FONTAINEBLEAU. Drawn by A. W. Lord.

89 CHURCH AT ORIZABA, MEX. Drawn by Denman W. Ross.

90 FIRST SKETCH FOR ST. JOHN'S CHURCH, FALL RIVER, MASS. Wheelwright & Haven, Architects.

91 FIRST STUDY FOR DEDHAM INN. Wheelwright & Haven, Architects.

92 STABLE FOR S. D. WARREN, MATTAPOISETT, MASS. Wheelwright & Haven, Architects.

93 INTERIOR. By John Zettel, Architect.

94 FAÇADE OF THE DUOMO SAN MARTINO, LUCCA. Drawn by J. Linden Smith.

95 THE COLEONI MONUMENT, VENICE. Drawn by J. Linden Smith.

96 SKETCHES OF CINCINNATI COLONIAL WORK. John Zettel.

97 TOWER OF S. M. IN COSMEDIN, ROME. Drawn by A. W. Lord.

98 ARCH OF THE MONEY-CHANGERS, ROME. Drawn by A. W. Lord.

99 VASE IN BRITISH MUSEUM, LONDON. Drawn by A. W. Lord.

100 CHURCH OF EL CARMEN, ORIZABA, MEX. Drawn by Denman W. Ross.

101 HOUSE AT IPSWICH, MASS. Jas. T. Kelley, Architect.

102 DESIGN FOR OFFICE BUILDING. Jas. T. Kelley, Architect.

103 FIRST NATIONAL BANK, LYNN, MASS. Jas. T. Kelley, Architect.

104 PORCH OF C. W. PORTER'S HOUSE, LYNN, MASS. Jas. T. Kelley, Architect.

105 BREWSTER ACADEMY, WOLFBORO', N.H. Jas. T. Kelley, Architect.

106 DESIGN FOR BILL-POSTER FOR BOSTON ARCHITECTURAL CLUB. H. P. Kirby.

107 A LITTLE MOUNTAIN CHURCH. E. Eldon Deane, Architect.

108 OLD STREET, PLYMOUTH, MASS. Drawn by H. C. Dunham.

109 CARPENTER'S HALL, PHILADELPHIA. Drawn by H. G. Ripley.

110 DESIGN FOR OPERA-HOUSE. C. H. Blackall, Architect. Drawn by A. H. Wright.

111 MISSION CHAPEL, EWING ST., CHICAGO. Irving K. Pond & Allen B. Pond, Architects.

112 DESIGN FOR METHODIST CHURCH, READING, PA. Mellen, Kirby, & Westell, Architects.

113 HALL OF ROBBINS MEMORIAL LIBRARY, ARLINGTON, MASS. Cabot, Everett, & Mead, Architects.

114 DESIGN FOR CITY CHURCH. P. G. Gulbranson, Architect.

115 ALTAR IN SAN BIAGIO, DUOMO, PISA. Drawn by Edgar A. Josselyn.

116 DESIGN FOR A LIBRARY, SCHOOL, AND HALL. Chas. T. Mott, Architect.

117 HOMESTEAD AT SYOSSET, L.I. Harrison Albright, Architect.

118 VESTIBULE OF HOTEL DE BEAUVAIS, PARIS. Drawn by C. H. Blackall.

119 RESIDENCE FOR MR. H. W. SMITH, BANGOR, ME. Edward T. Hapgood, Architect.

120 DESIGN FOR TROY ORPHAN ASYLUM. H. L. Warren, Architect.

121 INTERIOR OF NEW YORK CLUB-HOUSE. Lamb & Rich, Architects.

122 INTERIOR. H. T. Schladermundt, Designer.

123 THE CHEW HOUSE, GERMANTOWN, PA. Drawn by H. G. Ripley.

124 THREE HOUSES AT BROOKLINE, MASS. Cram & Wentworth, Architects.

125 HOUSE ON ASTOR STREET, CHICAGO. Irving K. Pond & Allen B. Pond, Architects.

126 HOUSE AND STABLE, SO. BETHLEHEM, PA. Wilson Eyre, Architect.

127 BAPTISMAL FONT IN THE CHURCH OF ST. JOHN THE DIVINE, VARICK ST., N.Y. Measured and drawn by S. Stevens Haskell.

128 HOUSE TO BE BUILT AT SOUTHPORT, LONG ISLAND SOUND. Wilson Eyre, Architect.

129 DESIGN FOR STAINED GLASS WINDOW. Phipps, Slocum, & Co.

130 THE MEYER GATES, HARVARD COLLEGE. Drawn by T. F. Walsh.

131 CARVED OAK CABINET. By I. Kirchmyer. Exhibited by Irving & Casson.

132 TOWER AT VENDOME, FRANCE. Drawn by H. Bacon.

133 CAMPANILE AND APSE OF THE CHURCH OF THE INCARNATION, DALLAS, TEX. B. G. Goodhue, Architect.

134 FOUNTAIN AT PRATO, ITALY. Drawn by Geo. F. Newton.

135 OLD MILL AT LE MANS, FRANCE. Drawn by H. B. Pennell.

136 HOTEL ALTEMONTE, STAUNTON, VA. Yarnall & Goforth, Architects.

137 VENETIAN WELL-CURB. Drawn by A. Kahn.

138 INTERIOR OF COLOGNE CATHEDRAL. Drawn by William H. Bailey.

139 OLD HOUSE, WERNIGERODE, GERMANY. Drawn by Frank A. Hays.

140 CARVED PANEL. By I. Kirchmyer. Exhibited by Irving & Casson.

141 OLD ROGER MORRIS MANSION, NEW YORK. Drawn by Edward H. Hoyt.

142 HOUSE IN FLORIDA. A. W. Cobb, Architect.

143 DORMER FROM CHATEAU DE BLOIS. Drawn by C. Bryant Schaefer.

144 PROPOSED HOTEL AT LAKE GEORGE, N.Y. Frank T. Corneil, Architect.

145 INTERIOR. Drawn by Geo. P. Fernald.

146 DESIGN FOR HALL MANTEL. By Robt. W. Jackson. First mention in B.A. Club competition.

147 COLONIAL DOORWAY. Drawn by S. Robinson.

148 Y.M.C.A. BUILDING, KALAMAZOO, MICH. Mason & Rice, Architects.

149 A SKETCH. By E. F. Maher.

150 RESIDENCE FOR ORIN SCOTTEN, DETROIT, MICH. John Scott & Co., Architects.

151 PRAY BUILDING, BOSTON. Winslow & Wetherell, Architects.

152 SHREVE, CRUMP, & LOW BUILDING, BOSTON. Winslow & Wetherell, Architects.

153 WALKER BUILDING, BOSTON. Winslow & Wetherell, Architects.

154 HOUSE FOR E. D. JORDAN, JR., COREY HILL, BROOKLINE. Winslow & Wetherell, Architects.

155 FAÇADE OF NEW BUILDING FOR AMERICAN FINE ARTS SOCIETY, N.Y. Design selected in competition. H. J. Hardenburgh, W. C. Hunting, and J. C. Jacobson, Architects.

156 INTERIOR OF ST. GEREON, COLOGNE. Drawn by Arthur Rotch.

157 LIMBURG CATHEDRAL. Drawn by Arthur Rotch.

158 COMPETITIVE DESIGN FOR BUILDING FOR MONTREAL BOARD OF TRADE. Rotch & Tilden, Architects.

159 ACCEPTED PRELIMINARY SKETCHES FOR ALL SAINTS' CHURCH, Dorchester, Mass. Cram & Wentworth, Architects.

160 GATEWAY TO UNIVERSITY, HUY, BELGIUM. Drawn by W. W. Bosworth.

161 PRESBYTERIAN CHURCH, OMAHA, NEB. Walker & Kimball, Architects.

162 ST. JAMES' CHURCH, PROVIDENCE, R.I. Walker & Kimball, Architects.

163 MT. VERNON CHURCH, BOSTON. Walker & Kimball, Architects.

164 DESIGN FOR WALNUT-ST. CHURCH, BROOKLINE, MASS. Walker & Kimball, Architects.

165 HOUSE FOR T. E. STILLMAN, Esq., MYSTIC, CONN. Walker & Kimball, Architects.

166 INTERIOR WORK. Photographed and Exhibited by Edwin H. Lincoln.

167 INTERIOR WORK. Photographed and Exhibited by Edwin H. Lincoln.

168 FLOWER STUDIES. Photographed and Exhibited by Edwin H. Lincoln.

169 HANCOCK CONGREGATIONAL CHURCH, LEXINGTON, MASS. Lewis & Paine, Architects.

170 SKETCHES NEAR HARTFORD, CONN. By W. S. Wells.

171 SKETCHES NEAR HARTFORD, CONN. By W. S. Wells.

172 STUDY FOR Y.M.C.A. BUILDING, WITTENBERG COLLEGE, SPRINGFIELD, O. Aiken & Ketcham, Architects.

173 SKETCH FOR TWELVE-ROOM SCHOOL BUILDING, FORT WAYNE, IND. Wing & Mahvrin, Architects.

174 OLD HOUSES AT ASKRIGG, YORKSHIRE, ENG. Drawn by H. B. Warren.

175 WALBURN HALL, NEAR RICHMOND, YORKSHIRE, ENG. Drawn by H. B. Warren.

176 READING LECTERN IN FIRST CONGREGATIONAL CHURCH, DETROIT, MICH. John Lyman Faxon, Architect.

177 COMMUNION TABLE FOR FIRST CONGREGATIONAL CHURCH, DETROIT, MICH. John Lyman Faxon, Architect.

178 CENTRAL BAPTIST CHURCH, NORWICH, CONN. John Lyman Faxon, Architect.

179 TOWN HALL, BARRINGTON, R.I. Stone, Carpenter, & Wilson, Architects.

180 BEDROOM FOR HENRY G. RUSSELL, Esq. Stone, Carpenter, & Wilson, Architects.

181 MEMORIAL HALL AT PETERSHAM, R.I. Stone, Carpenter, & Wilson, Architects.

182 MANTELS IN HOUSE AT PROVIDENCE, R.I. Stone, Carpenter, & Wilson, Architects.

183 TOWN HALL, BARRINGTON, R.I. PLANS. Stone, Carpenter, & Wilson, Architects.

184 TOWN HALL, BARRINGTON, R.I. ELEVATION. Stone, Carpenter, & Wilson, Architects.

185 SKETCHES FOR HOUSE AT PETERSHAM, R.I. Stone, Carpenter, & Wilson, Architects.

186 WATER COLOR. By J. H. McGuire.

187 DURER'S HOUSE, NUREMBERG. Drawn by Frederick P. Hill.

188 WATER COLOR, ROME. By Frederick P. Hill.

189 TOWER OF S. M. IN COSMEDIN, ROME. Drawn by Frederick P. Hill.

190 HOUSE AT SETAUKET, LONG ISLAND. C. A. Gifford, Architect.

191 SKETCH FOR WALL DECORATION. By Leake & Greene.

192 ARCH OF TITUS, ROME. Drawn by A. W. Lord.

193 GATEWAY OF THE CERTOSA, PAVIA. Drawn by A. W. Lord.

194 ARCH OF TITUS, ROME. Drawn by J. H. McGuire.

195 S. GIORGIO IN VELABRO, ROME. Drawn by J. H. McGuire.

196 LISIEUX. Drawn from Photograph by B. F. Mitchell.

197 FROM ATHENS. Drawn by J. J. W. Bradney.

198 A SEA-SHORE COTTAGE. L. G. Dittoe, Architect.

199 CINCINNATI ARCHITECTURAL CLUB COMPETITION. A WAREHOUSE. By Geo. E. Field.

200 THE WALDORF, NEW YORK. H. J. Hardenbergh, Architect.

201 A HOTEL. THESIS DRAWING, M.I.T. PLAN. By Frederick N. Reed.

202 A HOTEL. THESIS DRAWING, M.I.T. ELEVATION. By Frederick N. Reed.

203 SKETCH FOR A CLUB-HOUSE. Robert Coit, Architect.

204 DESIGN FOR THE ENTRANCE TO A CAVE. By Miss Alice Edson.

205 COMPETITIVE DESIGN FOR LOWELL CITY HALL. By Merrill & Cutler.

206 SKETCH DESIGNS. Lewis & Paine, Architects.

207 MURAL DECORATION IN CHRIST'S CHURCH, SAVANNAH, GA. By L. Haberstroh & Son.

208 DESIGN FOR THE NEW YORK CATHEDRAL. PLAN. John Lyman Faxon, Architect.

209 DESIGN FOR THE NEW YORK CATHEDRAL. PRINCIPAL FAÇADE. John Lyman Faxon, Architect.

210 COLORED MOSAICS, MONREALE CATHEDRAL. Drawn by John Lyman Faxon.

211 INTERIOR OF S. VITALE, RAVENNA. Drawn by John Lyman Faxon.

212 DETAIL OF ENTRANCE TO CRYPT. SAN ZENO, VERONA. Drawn by H. B. Warren.

213 BRONZE STATUE OF AN ATHLETE. Drawn from a print by W. J. Clark.

214 STAINED GLASS WINDOW IN BARGELLO MUSEUM, FLORENCE. Drawn by Geo. F. Newton.

215 VAN RENSSELAER MANOR HOUSE, ALBANY, N.Y. Measured and drawn by Wm. H. Orchard.

216 HOUSE AT CHESTNUT HILL, MASS. Edward Little Rogers, Architect.

217 INTERIOR OF FIRST CONGREGATIONAL CHURCH, DETROIT, MICH. John Lyman Faxon, Architect.

218 DESIGN. H. P. Kirby, Architect.

219 A SIDEBOARD. H. P. Kirby, Architect.

220 A SKETCH FOR A COUNTRY TAVERN. H. P. Kirby, Architect.

221 A COUNTRY HOTEL. Mellen, Westell, & Kirby. Architects.

222 A COMPOSITION. By H. P. Kirby.

223 A DORMER. H. P. Kirby, Architect.

224 FRIEZE ORNAMENT. Drawn by Chas. B. Bachmann.

225 AUPPEGARD, NORMANDY. Drawn by Chas. B. Bachmann.

226 HOUSE AT CHESTNUT HILL. Chapman & Frazer, Architects.

227 HOUSE AT WEST NEWTON, MASS. Chapman & Frazer, Architects.

228 HOUSE FOR HON. J. F. ANDREW, HINGHAM, MASS. Longfellow, Alden, & Harlow, Architects.

229 DESIGN FOR CARNEGIE LIBRARY, ALLEGHENY CITY, PA. John Lyman Faxon, Architect.

230 DESIGN FOR HALL DECORATION. By L. F. Perry.

231 CONVENT OF ST. OURS, AOSTA. Drawn by H. B. Warren.

232 TOWER OF THE GREY FRIARS, RICHMOND, YORKSHIRE. Drawn by H. B. Warren.

233 INTERIOR OF MANCHESTER CATHEDRAL. Drawn by H. B. Warren.

234 A PAVILION FOR A STATUE OF ZEUS. Gold medal, Architectural League of New York, 1890. By Howard Magonigle.

235 MURAL DECORATIONS. L. Haberstroh & Son.

236 DESIGN FOR NEW YORK CATHEDRAL. PERSPECTIVE. John Lyman Faxon, Architect.

237 DESIGNS FOR FURNITURE. By Edgar A. Somes, for Keeler & Co.

238 DECORATIONS IN FIRST PARISH CHURCH, WAKEFIELD, MASS. By L. Haberstroh.

239 PORCH TO HOUSE IN LONGWOOD, MASS. E. A. P. Newcomb, Architect.

240 HOUSE AT WOBURN, MASS. E. A. P. Newcomb, Architect.

241 HOUSE AT LONGWOOD, MASS. E. A. P. Newcomb, Architect.

242 HOUSE ON BEACON STREET, BROOKLINE, MASS. E. A. P. Newcomb, Architect.

243 SKETCH CLUB OF NEW YORK. MONTHLY COMPETITION. Designs by J. A. Johnson, Julius Harder.

244 COTTAGE NEAR STRATFORD, ENGLAND. Drawn by Frank A. Hays.

245 HAMILTON HOUSE, PHILADELPHIA. Drawn by Frank A. Hays.

246 RESIDENCE OF MR. CHAS. A. SACKETT, NEW LONDON, CONN. Geo. Warren Cole, Architect.

247 RESIDENCES AT ORANGE, N.J. Rossiter & Wright, Architects.

248 STUDY FOR A CITY HOUSE. C. Burton Keen, Architect.

249 OLD BELL GABLE, LOS ANGELES, CAL. Drawn by C. Burton Keen.

250 WATCH TOWER AND GATEWAY, LUCCA, ITALY. Drawn by C. Burton Keen.

251 FRENCH COTTAGE. E. L. Simmons.

252 OLD STATE HOUSE, BOSTON. Drawn by Clement Remington.

253 ST. MARTIN'S EPISCOPAL CHURCH. Harrison Albright, Architect.

254 SEA-SHORE COTTAGE. Arthur Stedman, Delineator and Designer.

255 NEW GERMAN OPERA-HOUSE, CHICAGO. Adler & Sullivan, Architects.

256 RESIDENCE OF DR. JAS. E. GARRETSON, LANSDOWNE, PA. Harrison Albright, Architect.

257 FOUNTAIN TO BE ERECTED AT HOLLISTON, MASS. W. L. Walker.

258 DOORWAY IN ST. MARY'S CHURCH, SHREWSBURY, ENG. Drawn by M. H. Bancroft.

259 DESIGN FOR TROY ORPHAN ASYLUM. H. L. Warren.

260 RESTORATION OF LAVATORY IN CLOISTER, WENLOCK PRIORY. Drawn by H. L. Warren.

261 HOSPITAL AND REAR ENTRANCE ARCH, TROY ORPHAN ASYLUM. H. Langford Warren, Architect.

262 HOUSE OF S. A. ORR, Esq., TROY, N.Y. H. Langford Warren.

263 COMPOSITION. C. Bryant Schaefer.

264 A TOWER ON THE WALLS, NUREMBERG. Drawn by Irving K. Pond.

265 WINDOW OF REFECTORY, CHESTER CATHEDRAL. Drawn by M. H. Bancroft.

266 RESIDENCE FOR MR. JAMES CHAMLEY, CHICAGO. Adler & Sullivan.

267 ENTRANCE TO RESIDENCE LAKE SHORE DRIVE, CHICAGO. Irving K. Pond & Allen B. Pond, Architects.

268 MELROSE ABBEY, SOUTH ENTRANCE. Measured and drawn by H. B. Bare, F.R.I.B.A.

269 EASTERN BALCONY, ST. MARK'S, VENICE. Drawn by H. Bloomfield Bare, F.R.I.B.A.

270 SEVENTEENTH CENTURY CARVED OAK ALTAR TABLE, TOWNSTAL CHURCH, ENG. Drawn by H. Bloomfield Bare, F.R.I.B.A.

271 SKETCH FOR A COTTAGE. Wilson Eyre, Jr., Architect.

272 PENCIL STUDY. Wilson Eyre, Jr.

273 ROWALLAN CASTLE, AYRSHIRE. Drawn by E. L. Simmons.

274 STAIR NEWELL. SECOND MENTION, T SQUARE CLUB COMPETITION. J. P. Jamieson.

275 A 40-FOOT CLUB FRONT. T SQUARE CLUB COMPETITION. Adin Benedict Lacey.

276 WATER COLOR. W. H. Kilham.

277 HALL BAY WINDOW, MR. BURPEE RENNSEY'S HOUSE, LYNN. Jas. T. Kelley, Architect.

278 SKETCH FOR STAIRCASE WINDOW. Leake & Greene.

279 SKETCH FOR LIBRARY DECORATION. Leake & Greene.

280 SKETCH FOR LIBRARY WINDOW. Leake & Greene.

281 MURAL DECORATION. L. Haberstroh & Sons.

282 BELL IN TOWER, WORCESTER CATHEDRAL, ENG. Drawn by W. L. Baily.

283 OLD HOUSE IN BOURGES. Drawn by W. L. Baily.

284 CRYPT, MONT ST. MICHEL. Drawn by W. L. Baily.

285 VISP, SWITZERLAND. Drawn W. L. Baily.

286 WELLS CATHEDRAL, INTERIOR. Drawn by W. L. Baily.

287 L'ESCALIER DE LA REINE, CHARTRES. Drawn by W. L. Baily.

288 A STREET IN BRANDENBURG, GERMANY. Drawn by W. L. Baily.

289 DECORATION FROM SCHIESWERDERS HALL, BRESLAU. Drawn by C. E. Schermerhorn.

290 MR. LEE HAMMOND'S HOUSE, ALLSTON, MASS. Cram & Wentworth, Architects.

291 A HARBOR TOWER. SKETCH CLUB OF NEW YORK. FIRST PRIZE. J. Addison Johnson.

292 DESIGN FOR DECORATION OF SIDE OF PARLOR. L. F. Perry.

293 DESIGN FOR DECORATION OF CEILING. L. F. Perry.

294 PHOTOGRAPHS OF COLONIAL ARCHITECTURE. By James M. Corner and E. E. Soderholtz.

295 PHOTOGRAPHS OF COLONIAL ARCHITECTURE. By James M. Corner and E. E. Soderholtz.

296 PHOTOGRAPHS OF COLONIAL ARCHITECTURE. By James M. Corner and E. E. Soderholtz.

297 INTERIOR OF MOSQUE. Drawn by Mrs. A. J. Jacossey.

298 SKETCH FOR HOUSE AT BAR HARBOR. E. G. W. Dietrich.

299 PALACE HOTEL, GOSHEN, VA. Yarnall & Goforth, Architects.

300 ST. LAWRENCE CHURCH, NUREMBERG. Drawn by W. L. Baily.

301 HADDON PUBLIC SCHOOL, HADDONFIELD, N. J. Harrison Albright, Architect.

302 DESIGN FOR CITY HOUSE. Wheelwright & Haven, Architects.

303 DESIGN FOR GYMNASIUM. W. W. Bosworth, Architect.

304 DESIGN FOR GYMNASIUM. W. W. Bosworth, Architect.

305 MAGDALEN ASYLUM, N.Y. W. W. Bosworth, Architect.

306 MAGDALEN ASYLUM, N.Y. W. W. Bosworth, Architect.

307 DESIGN FOR AMERICAN FINE ARTS SOCIETY BUILDING. H. Langford Warren, Architect.

308 WENLOCK PRIORY. Measured and drawn by H. Langford Warren.

309 DESIGN FOR TROY ORPHAN ASYLUM. H. Langford Warren, Architect.

310 DESIGN FOR TROY ORPHAN ASYLUM. H. Langford Warren, Architect.

311 WENLOCK PRIORY. Measured and drawn by H. Langford Warren.

312 MURAL DECORATION. L. Haberstroh & Son.

313 MURAL DECORATION. L. Haberstroh & Son.

314 MURAL DECORATION. L. Haberstroh & Son.

315 CEILING DESIGN. L. Haberstroh & Son.

316 MURAL DECORATION. L. Haberstroh & Son.

317 MURAL DECORATIONS. L. Haberstroh & Son.

318 DESIGN FOR DECORATION OF PARLOR CEILING. L. F. Perry.

319 PHOTOGRAPH, INTERIOR, RESIDENCE OF MRS. HEARST, WASHINGTON, D.C. Harvey L. Page & Co., Architects.

320 INTERIOR, RESIDENCE OF MRS. HEARST, WASHINGTON, D.C. Harvey L. Page & Co., Architects.

321 PHOTOGRAPH OF INTERIOR MRS. HEARST'S RESIDENCE, WASHINGTON, D.C. Harvey L. Page & Co., Architects.

322 PHOTOGRAPH OF INTERIOR MRS. HEARST'S RESIDENCE, WASHINGTON, D.C. Harvey L. Page & Co., Architects.

323 PHOTOGRAPH OF INTERIOR MRS. HEARST'S RESIDENCE, WASHINGTON, D.C. Harvey L. Page & Co., Architects.

324 PHOTOGRAPH OF INTERIOR MRS. HEARST'S RESIDENCE, WASHINGTON, D.C. Harvey L. Page & Co., Architects.

325 PHOTOGRAPH OF INTERIOR MRS. HEARST'S RESIDENCE, WASHINGTON, D.C. Harvey L. Page & Co., Architects.

326 PHOTOGRAPH OF INTERIOR MRS. HEARST'S RESIDENCE, WASHINGTON, D.C. Harvey L. Page & Co., Architects.

327 PHOTOGRAPH OF INTERIOR MRS. HEARST'S RESIDENCE, WASHINGTON, D.C. Harvey L. Page & Co., Architects.

328 DESIGN FOR HOTEL, DETROIT. Donaldson & Meier, Architects.

329 CAMBRIDGE CITY HALL. Longfellow, Alden, & Harlow, Architects.

330 COMPETITIVE DESIGN FOR TOWN HALL. H. Langford Warren, Architect.

331 TOWN HALL, LINCOLN, MASS. H. Langford Warren, Architect.

332 PRIZE DRAWING. IONIC ORDER. George Carey.

333 TAPESTRY. By Leake & Greene.

334 TAPESTRY. By Leake & Greene.

335 DESIGN FOR PROPOSED MEMORIAL WINDOW, TRINITY CHAPEL, BOSTON. Edwin Ford and Frederick Brooks.

336 ALTERNATE FOR NO. 335.

337 ACCEPTED DESIGN FOR MEMORIAL WINDOW, BUFFALO, N.Y. Edwin Ford and Frederick Brooks.

338 ACCEPTED DESIGN FOR MEMORIAL WINDOW, CINCINNATI, O. Edwin Ford and Frederick Brooks.

339 ACCEPTED DESIGN FOR MEMORIAL WINDOW, ERIE, PA. Edwin Ford and Frederick Brooks.

340 ACCEPTED DESIGN FOR MEMORIAL WINDOW, PITTSFIELD, MASS. Edwin Ford and Frederick Brooks.

341 ACCEPTED DESIGN FOR MEMORIAL WINDOW, TROY, N.Y. Edwin Ford and Frederick Brooks.

342 ACCEPTED DESIGN FOR MEMORIAL WINDOW, TROY, N.Y. Edwin Ford and Frederick Brooks.

343 PERSPECTIVE VIEW OF MACHINERY HALL, WORLD'S COLUMBIAN EXPOSITION. Peabody & Stearns, Architects.

344 COLOR SCHEME FOR SAME.

345 to 352 incl. SCALE DRAWINGS OF SAME.

353 PERSPECTIVE VIEW OF MASSACHUSETTS HOUSE, WORLD'S COLUMBIAN EXPOSITION. Peabody & Stearns, Architects.

354 WEST FRONT, RESIDENCE OF HERBERT JAQUES, BROOKLINE. Andrews & Jaques, Architects.

355 RESIDENCE FOR W. FREDERICK SNYDER, CHELTEN HILLS, PA. Harrison Albright, Architect.

356 COUNTRY HOUSES. Loring & Phipps, Architects.

357 DESIGN FOR CLUB-HOUSE. Loring & Phipps, Architects.

358 DESIGN FOR MEMORIAL HALL AND HIGH SCHOOL. Loring & Phipps, Architects.

359 SCALE DETAILS, LYMAN GYMNASIUM, PROVIDENCE. Stone, Carpenter, & Wilson, Architects.

360 SCALE DETAILS, LYMAN GYMNASIUM, PROVIDENCE. Stone, Carpenter, & Wilson, Architects.

361 SCALE DETAILS, LYMAN GYMNASIUM, PROVIDENCE. Stone, Carpenter, & Wilson, Architects.

362 DESIGN FOR STAINED GLASS WINDOW. Phipps, Slocum, & Co.

363 DESIGN FOR STAINED GLASS WINDOW. Phipps, Slocum, & Co.

364 DESIGN FOR STAINED GLASS WINDOW. Phipps, Slocum, & Co.

365 DESIGN FOR STAINED GLASS WINDOW. Phipps, Slocum, & Co.

366 STAINED GLASS WINDOW DESIGN, "CHRIST BLESSING CHILDREN." Phipps, Slocum, & Co.

367 MEMORIAL TABLET, STAINED GLASS. Phipps, Slocum, & Co.

368 CARTOON FOR ST. MATTHEW'S LUTHERAN CHURCH, PHILA. Phipps, Slocum, & Co.

369 CARTOON FOR ST. MATTHEW'S LUTHERAN CHURCH, PHILA. Phipps, Slocum, & Co.

370 CARTOON FOR ST. MATTHEW'S LUTHERAN CHURCH, PHILA. Phipps, Slocum, & Co.

371 FRONT PORCH. Andrews, Jaques, & Rantoul, Architects. Drawn by W. S. Wells.

372 WOMAN'S BUILDING, WORLD'S COLUMBIAN EXPOSITION Second Prize. Miss Lois L. Howe, Jr., Architect.

373 WOMAN'S BUILDING, WORLD'S COLUMBIAN EXPOSITION. Miss Lois L. Howe, Jr., Architect.

374 KNIGHTS OF PYTHIAS TEMPLE, CLEVELAND, O. Cramer & Fugman, Architects.

375 OLD HOUSE, BEVERLY. W. H. Kilham.

376 RESIDENCE OF MR. MARSHALL S. MAHURIN, FORT WAYNE, IND. Wing & Mahurin, Architects.

377 COMPETITIVE DESIGN FOR INDIANA BUILDING, WORLD'S COLUMBIAN EXPOSITION. Wing & Mahurin, Architects.

378 COMPETITIVE DESIGN FOR INDIANA BUILDING, WORLD'S COLUMBIAN EXPOSITION. Wing & Mahurin, Architects.

379 COMPETITIVE DESIGN FOR INDIANA BUILDING, WORLD'S COLUMBIAN EXPOSITION. Wing & Mahurin, Architects.

380 INTERIORS. Stone, Carpenter, & Wilson.

381 GRANT MONUMENT. Geo. S. Keller, Architect.

382 PERSPECTIVE OF HOUSE FOR F. D. FISH, SOUTH BEND, IND. Charles Alling Gifford, Architect.

383 INTERIOR OF GRANT MONUMENT. Geo. S. Keller, Architect.

384 DESIGN FOR A GATE LODGE. Drawn by E. L. Simmons.

385 RESIDENCE OF W. W. NORTHEND, ARCHITECT, PHILLIPS BEACH, MASS.

386 PHOTOGRAPHS AND DRAWINGS, SHOWING FIRE-PROOF CONSTRUCTION. Guastavino Fire-proof Construction Co.

387 HOUSE OF R. D. ANDREWS, ARCHITECT, WELLESLEY FARMS, MASS.

388 DRAWINGS. By A. Kahn, American Architect Traveling Scholar.

389 DESIGNS FOR SCHOOL-HOUSES. Loring & Phipps, Architects.

390 SKETCHES AND DESIGN FOR CHURCH. Loring & Phipps, Architects.

391 DESIGNS FOR SCHOOL-HOUSES. Loring & Phipps, Architects.

392 RESIDENCE OF E. P. CARPENTER, MANCHESTER. E. A. P. Newcomb, Architect.

393 RESIDENCE OF E. W. ANTHONY, LONGWOOD. E. A. P. Newcomb, Architect.

394 THE DOOLY BLOCK AND HOTEL ONTARIO, SALT LAKE CITY. Adler & Sullivan, Architects.

395 STORES AND DWELLINGS AT DETROIT. Leon Coquorel, Architect.

396 PHOTOGRAPH OF ASSOCIATE REFORMED CHURCH, BALTIMORE. Charles C. Cassel, Architect.

397 DESIGN FOR SCHOOL-HOUSE, SOMERVILLE, MASS. Loring & Phipps, Architects.

398 COUNTRY HOUSE. Cook, Hapgood, & Co., Architects.

399 OLD WEIGHING HOUSE AT DEVENTER, HOLLAND. Drawn by Chas. H. Israels.

400 STABLE FOR J. A. MINOTT, SO. ORANGE, N.J. Rossiter & Wright, Architects.

401 WAINWRIGHT BUILDING, ST. LOUIS, MO. Adler & Sullivan, Architects.

402 PROPOSED HOME FOR NEWTON CLUB. Samuel J. Brown, Architect.

403 PROPOSED GYMNASIUM FOR STATE NORMAL SCHOOL, WEST CHESTER, PA. Harrison Albright, Architect.

404 RANDOLPH-MACON WOMAN'S COLLEGE, LYNCHBURG, VA. W. M. Poindexter, Architect.

405 DESIGN FOR HOTEL AND OPERA-HOUSE. C. H. Blackall, Architect.

406 A ROOM FROM THE STABIAN BATHS, POMPEII. Drawn by G. F. Newton.

407 OWLS' NEST COUNTRY CLUB, SAN CARLOS, CAL. Willis Polk & Fritz Gamble, Architects.

408 HOUSE NEAR SHREWSBURY, ENG. Drawn by G. F. Newton.

409 OLD HOUSE AT ROTHENBURG, GERMANY. Drawn by Lloyd Titus.

410 CHURCH TOWER. Drawn by C. G. Vierheiling.

411 UNIVERSITY COTTAGE CLUB, PRINCETON, N.J. Ross & Marvin, Architects.

412 OLD HOUSE AT FORT MIFFLIN, BELOW PHILADELPHIA. Drawn by Lloyd Titus.

413 DESIGN FOR A FOUR-ROOM SCHOOL-HOUSE. Wing & Mahurin, Architects.

414 LIBRARY OF ST. MARK'S, VENICE. Measured and drawn by S. W. Meade.

415 CLOCK TOWER, CHARTRES CATHEDRAL. Measured and drawn by S. W. Meade.

416 PORCH OF CHURCH AT ST. GILLES. Measured and drawn by S. W. Meade.

417 PORTION OF THE FAÇADE OF THE CHATEAU AT CHENONCEAU, FRANCE. Measured and drawn by Geo. F. Newton.

418 CEILING FROM THE CHAPEL IN THE RICARDI PALACE, FLORENCE. Measured and drawn by Geo. F. Newton.

419 MOSAICS FROM THE CATHEDRAL BAPTISTRY AT RAVENNA, ITALY. Measured and drawn by G. F. Newton.

420 CAMPANILE OF ANGOULEME CATHEDRAL, FRANCE. Measured and drawn by G. F. Newton.

421 TOMB IN MEDICI CHAPEL, FLORENCE. Measured and drawn by Lyman Sise.

422 ISLEBORO INN. Wheelwright & Haven, Architects.

423 HOUSES AT TROY, N.Y. H. Langford Warren, Architect.

424 GENERAL VIEW OF HOUSE OF C. E. PATTERSON, Esq., TROY, N.Y. H. Langford Warren, Architect.

425 MAIN PORCH OF SAME.

426 PRIVATE DOOR OF SAME.

427 PENCIL SKETCHES IN SOUTH KENSINGTON MUSEUM. By R. C. Spencer, Jr.

428 PENCIL SKETCHES IN SOUTH KENSINGTON MUSEUM. By R. C. Spencer, Jr.

429 REDESDALE HALL, MORETON-ON-MARSH. Ernest, George, & Peto, Architects. Loaned by the Boston Architectural Club.

430 HOTEL CLUNY, PARIS, FAÇADE TOWARD THE COURT. Measured and drawn by Henry Bacon, Jr.

431 TOMB OF THE MARGRAVE HUGO, FLORENCE. Measured and drawn by Henry Bacon.

432 WATER COLOR, VENICE. Drawn by H. Bacon.

433 CORNICE OF THE RICARDI PALACE. Drawn by H. Bacon.

434 DOORWAY OF CATHEDRAL, VERONA. Drawn by H. Bacon.

435 S. MARIA, TOSCANELLA. Drawn by H. Bacon.

436 S. BARTOLOMMEO, PISTOJA. Drawn by H. Bacon.

437 STAIRCASE TOWER, BOURGES. Drawn by H. Bacon.

438 APSE OF ST. PIERRE, CAEN. Drawn by H. Bacon.

439 PENCIL SKETCHES, VENICE. Drawn by H. Bacon.

440 FONTAINE DES INNOCENTS, PARIS. Drawn by H. Bacon.

441 HOTEL DE LA MONNAIE, CAEN. Drawn by H. Bacon.

442 CLOISTER AT ARLES. Drawn by H. Bacon.

443 HOUSE OF ARTHUR LITTLE, ARCHITECT, BOSTON, MASS. Drawn by J. P. Fernald.

444 CUMBERLAND PRESBYTERIAN CHURCH, ST. LOUIS, MO. Chas. E. Illsley, Architect.

445 PUBLIC BUILDING. Chas. E. Illsley, Architect.

446 WALL DECORATIONS FROM THE ALHAMBRA. Drawn by E. A. Josselyn.

447 THE CA D'ORO, VENICE. Drawn by E. A. Josselyn.

448 CHURCH AT SCEAUX. Drawn by E. A. Josselyn.

449 FOREIGN SKETCHES. By E. A. Josselyn.

450 FOREIGN SKETCHES. By E. A. Josselyn.

451 MOSAIC WORK, FLORENCE. Drawn by E. A. Josselyn.

452 GENERAL VIEW OF COREY HILL, BROOKLINE, MASS. Drawn by H. B. Pennell.

453 DESIGN FOR SIOUX CITY HIGH SCHOOL. A. L. Darrow and R. H. Miller, Architects.

House to be built at
Southport Long Island Sound
Wilson Eyre
Arch.
Philadelphia

DESIGN FOR BILL-POSTER FOR BOSTON ARCHITECTURAL CLUB.

By H. P. Kirby.

+ A Little Mountain Church +
E. Eldon Deane . Architect.
Boston Mass .

DESIGN FOR BUILDING FOR A.M. FINE ARTS SOCIETY N.Y.

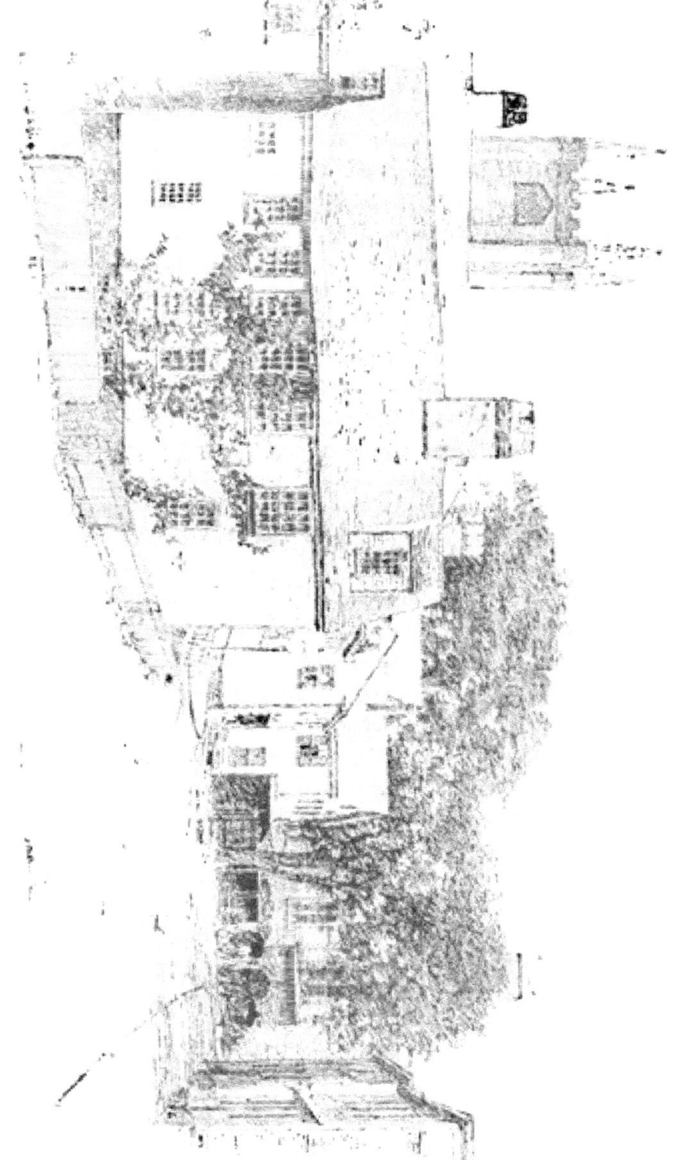

CARPENTERS HALL.
(REAR VIEW.) PHILADELPHIA

SALEM OPERA HOUSE

THE ENTRANCE

DRAWN BY

MISSION CHAPEL. EWING STREET CHICAGO.
IRVING K. POND & ALLEN B. POND ARCHITECTS.

DESIGN FOR METHODIST CHURCH, READING, PA.

Mellen, Kirby, and Westell, Architects.

DESIGN FOR TROY ORPHAN ASYLUM. H. L. WARREN, ARCHITECT.

* Grand Hall *

H T. SCHLADERMUNDT
Architectural. Decorator.

H T. SCHLADERMUNDT
Architectural. Decorator,

THE CHEW HOUSE
Germantown, Pennsylvania

THE HOVSE OF EVGENE FELLNER, ESQ on *Aspinwall* Hill Brookline Massachusetts ∞ Messrs Cram and Wentworth whose *Office* is at *Number* 53 *State Street* being the Architects

ON ASTOR STREET CHICAGO
IRVING K POND & ALLEN B POND ARCHITECTS

HOUSE & STABLE
SOUTH BETHLEHEM PA
HALL
LIBRARY
PORCH
TERRACE
CARRIAGES

Baptismal Font in the Church of Saint John the Devine

Varick Street New York City

Measured and Drawn September 1851 by

S. Stevens Haskell.

A PROPOSED HOTEL
AT LAKE GEORGE N.Y.
154 NOBLE ST. BROOKLYN

DORMER FROM CHATEAU DE BLOIS.

Drawn by C. Bryant Schaefer.

DESIGN FOR HALL MANTEL. BY ROBERT W. JACKSON.

FIRST MENTION IN B. A. CLUB COMPETITION.

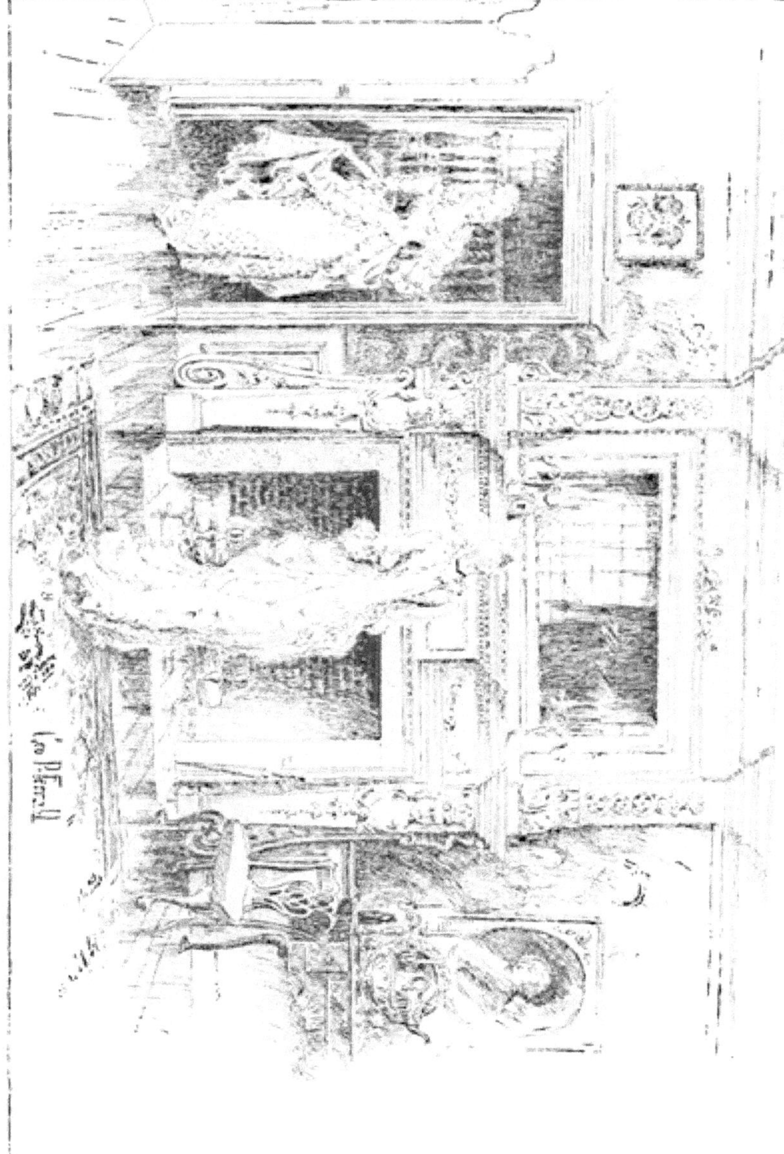

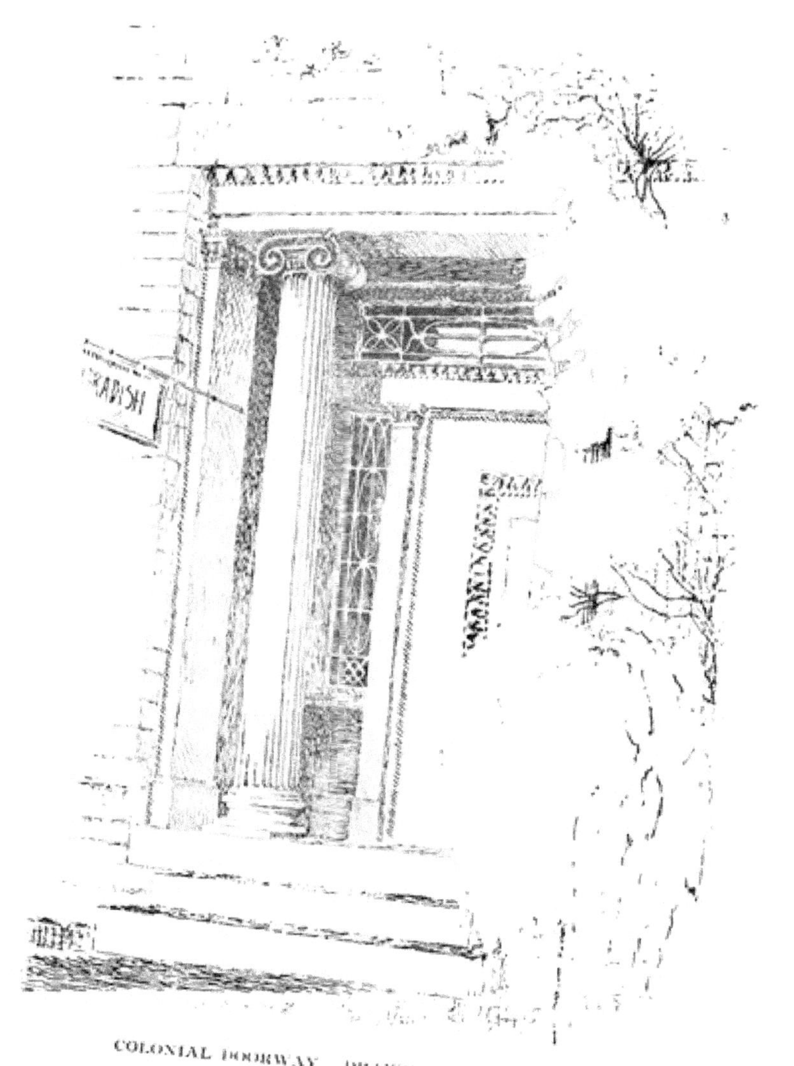

COLONIAL DOORWAY. DRAWN BY S. ROBINSON.

SCOTTEN

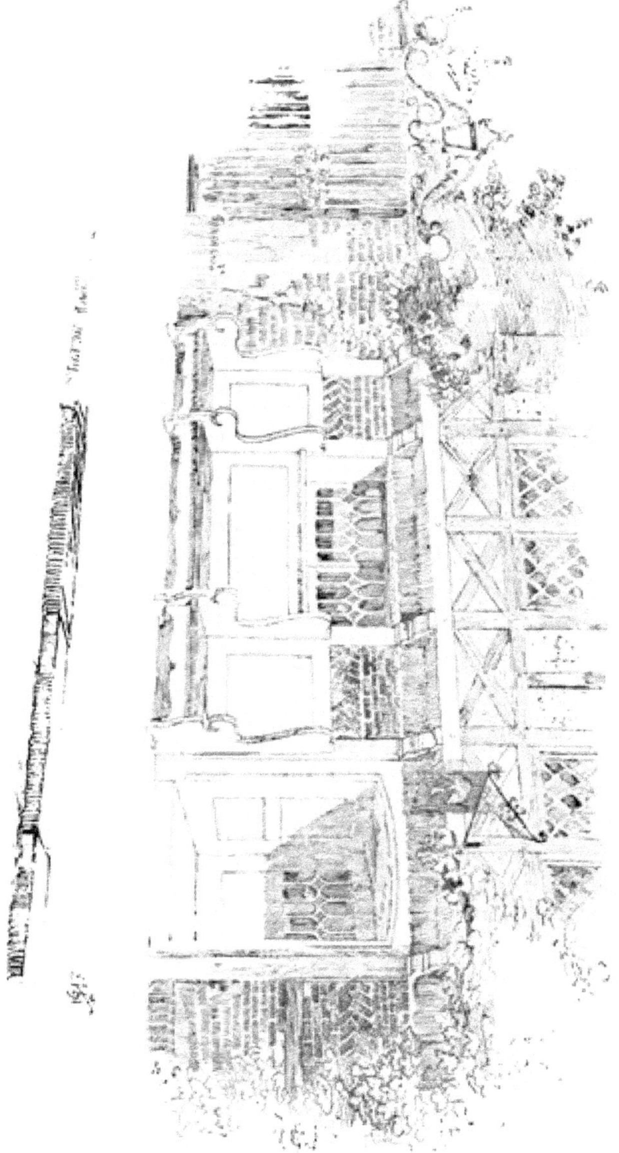

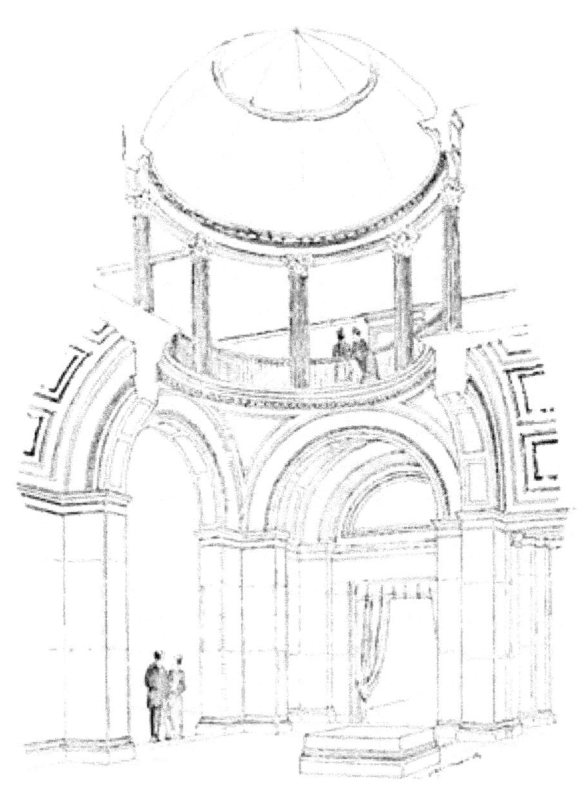

· HALL ·

ROBBINS MEMORIAL LIBRARY
ARLINGTON MASS

CABOT EVERETT AND MEAD · ARCHTS

DESIGN FOR A CITY CHURCH. BY P. G. GULBRANSON.

·ALTAR·OF·S·BIAGIO·
·DUOMO·PISA·

ALTERNATIVE
DESIGN

Proposed Building for a Library School and Hall
to be erected in [illegible]

[illegible] Archt
[illegible] Broadway NY City

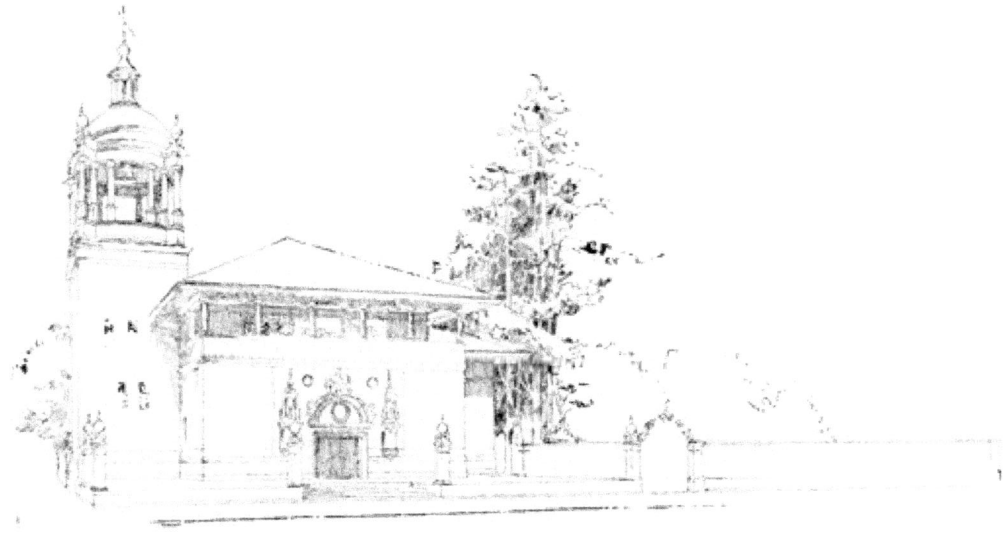

PHILADELPHIA PA.

VESTIBULE OF HOTEL DE BEAUVAIS, PARIS.

Drawn by C. H. Blackall.

RESIDENCE · FOR ·
MR · H·W· SMITH · BANGOR · ME ·
EDW · T · HAPGOOD · ARCH'T · NEW · YORK ·

Sketch from Photo
Pennell
Le Mans.

VENETIAN WELL CURB. DRAWN BY A. KAHN.

INTERIOR OF COLOGNE CATHEDRAL.

Drawn by Wm. H. Baily.

Frank A Hays -91-

Old house, Wernigerode-Germany

CARVED PANEL. BY I. KIRCHMYER.

Exhibited by Irving and Casson.

·OLD·ROGER·MORRIS·
·MANSION··· NEW·YORK·
·EDWARD·H·HOYT·DEL·
1 8 9 1

DESIGNED AND DRAWN BY A. W. COBB, ARCHITECT.

DESIGN FOR STAINED GLASS WINDOW.

Phipps, Slocum, & Co.

THE MEYER GATES, HARVARD COLLEGE. DRAWN BY T. F. WALSH.

Aug 24 1889

Campanile & Apse of
The Church of the Incarnation
Dallas Texas

Bertram G Goodhue Arch't

FOUNTAIN AT PRATO, ITALY. DRAWN BY G. F. NEWTON.

DESIGN FOR STAINED GLASS WINDOW. BY FORD AND BROOKS.

MAIN ENTRANCE
TEMPLE·BETH·EL·
FIFTH AVE & 76th STREET
NEW YORK
BRUNNER & TRYON
ARCHITECTS

INDEX TO ADVERTISERS

Alphabetical List of Advertisers

Shreve, Crump & Low Co.

Gas and Electric Fixtures.

Two entire floors are devoted to this department of our business, and we are prepared to meet any demand for

Low Priced,

Medium Quality,

OR THE

Most Expensive

Gas and Electric Fixtures

From original designs, and in keeping with the latest features of decoration.

The attention of Architects and clients is respectfully called to our original designs as shown by drawings in this exhibition.

SHREVE, CRUMP & LOW CO.,

MANUFACTURERS.

147 Tremont, Cor. West St., Boston.

SOLE AGENTS FOR THE

ARCHER & PANCOAST MFG. COMPANY OF NEW YORK.

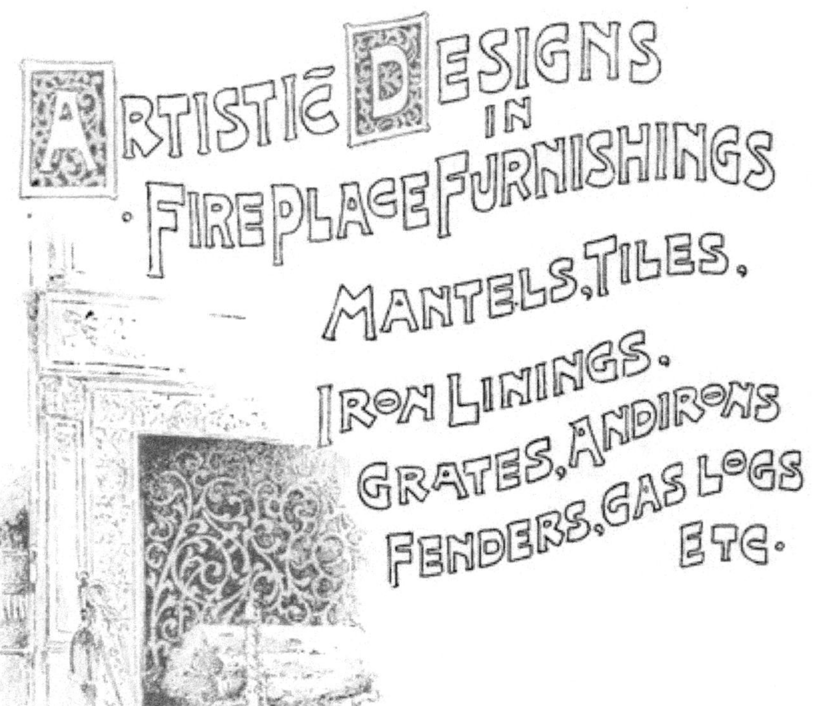

GEO. E. CRAWLEY.

171 TREMONT ST.

COR. MASON ST.

BOSTON MASS

MUSIC ROOM WINDOW IN "MARCHMONT."
Residence of Joseph N. White, Esq., Winchendon, Mass.

THE

HABERSTROH DECORATIVE PROCESS,

(Patented in the United States, Great Britain, Canada, and France)

IS A THOROUGHLY ARTISTIC AND REFINED METHOD FOR PRODUCING DELICATE SURFACES ON

CEILINGS AND WALLS.

DESIGNS AND COLORINGS SPECIALLY MADE TO CONFORM WITH THE ARCHITECTURE AND CONDITIONS OF THE BUILDING OR ROOM, WITH THE IDEA OF HARMONIZING THE EFFECT OF DETAILS. DESIGNS AND ESTIMATES FURNISHED, AND WORK EXECUTED IN ANY PART OF THE UNITED STATES.

REPRODUCTIONS

OF TAPESTRIES, EMBOSSED LEATHER, MOSAICS, AND TEXTILE FABRICS.

PAPIER MACHÉ, CARTON PIERRE, AND PLASTIC RELIEF DECORATIONS.

L. HABERSTROH & SON DEL.

A. McKenney & Co.
MAKERS OF FIXTVRES FOR ELECTRIC & GAS LIGHT
THE HIGHEST ARTISTIC TALENT combined with skilled Artizanship enable us to produce the most advanced & correct Styles of Fixtures for Artificial Lighting. A visit to our spacious and best appointed Show Parlors will convince you
634 636 Washington str BOSTON
VAN DYCK
LE BRUN
ROMA
KAROLOS MAGNO
XIX

Carnegie, Phipps & Co., Limited,

PITTSBURGH, PA.

Manufacturers of

STEEL AND IRON BEAMS
CHANNELS, ANGLES,
PLATES, &C.

BOSTON OFFICE.
3 MASON BUILDING.

GEO. H. WIGHTMAN,
N. E. AGENT

"CLINTON" DOUBLE TWIST WARP.

"CLINTON" STIFFENED AND CORRUGATED

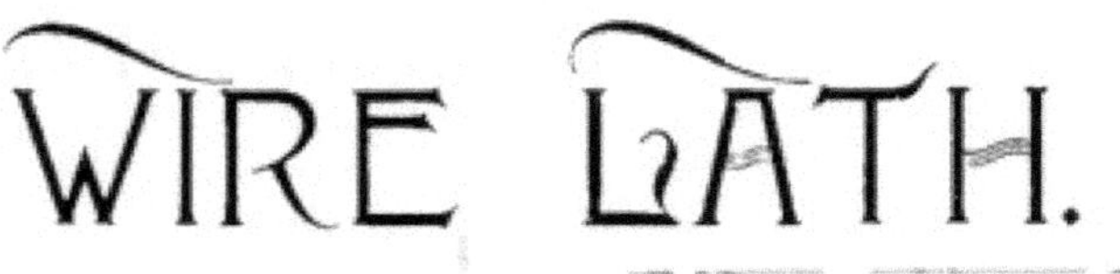

CLINTON WIRE CLOTH CO.

PATENTEES AND SOLE MANUFACTURERS OF THE ABOVE-NAMED LATH.

MOST PERFECT AND ECONOMIC SYSTEM OF FIRE-PROOF CONSTRUCTION.

Ceilings Plastered on this Lath will Never Crack.

SEND FOR CIRCULARS.

FACTORY:
CLINTON, MASS.

76 BEEKMAN STREET, NEW YORK.
501 SEARS BUILDING, BOSTON.
137 LAKE STREET, CHICAGO.

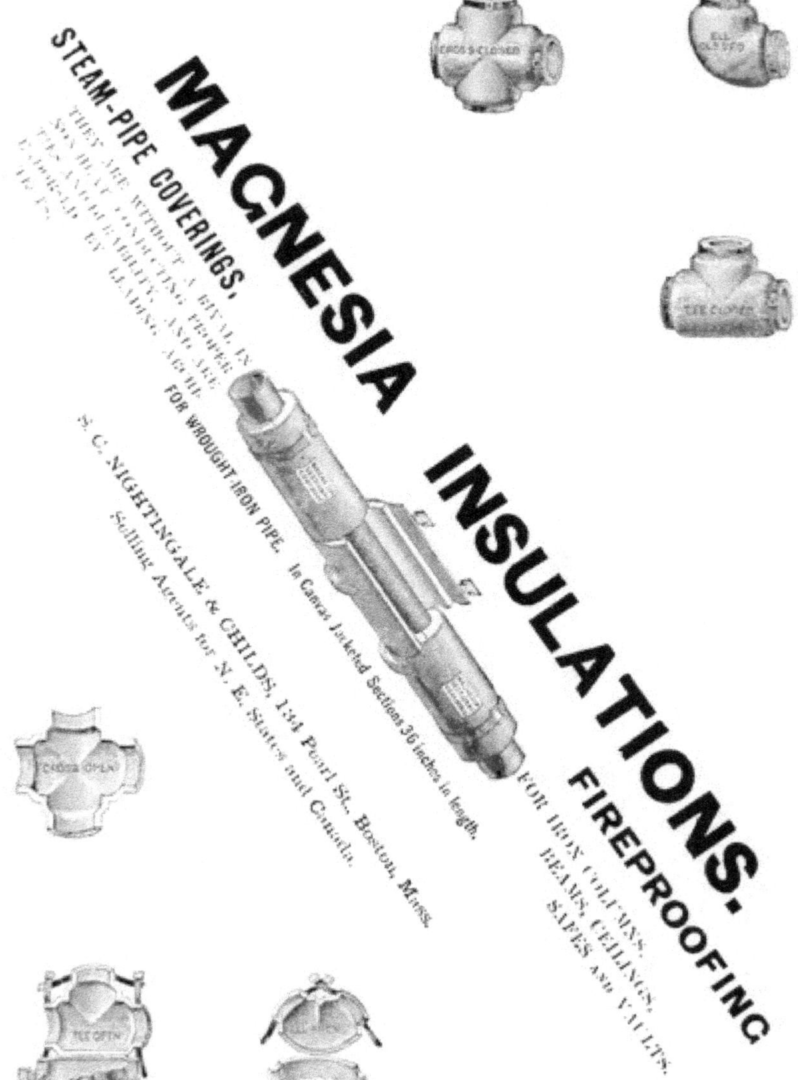
MAGNESIA INSULATIONS.
STEAM-PIPE COVERINGS,
FOR WROUGHT-IRON PIPE. In Canvas Jacketed Sections 36 inches in length.
FIREPROOFING
FOR IRON COLUMNS, BEAMS, CEILINGS, SAFES AND VAULTS.
S. C. NIGHTINGALE & CHILDS, 134 Pearl St., Boston, Mass.
Selling Agents for N. E. States and Canada.
CROSS CLOSED
ELL CLOSED
TEE CLOSED
CROSS OPEN
TEE OPEN

THE NORTON DOOR-CHECK AND SPRING

Closes Doors without Slamming or Breaking of Glass.

AGENTS.

H. A. BERRY, 39 DEY STREET, NEW YORK, N.Y.;
ORR & LOCKETT HARDWARE CO., 184 CLARK STREET, CHICAGO, ILL.;
PICKERING HARDWARE CO., MAIN AND FIFTH STREET, CINCINNATI, O.;
JAS. MORTON & SON, 1511 DODGE STREET, OMAHA, NEB.;
F. D. MORRELL, 224 MARKET STREET, SAN FRANCISCO, CAL.;
C. SCHNEIDER, 1205 F STREET, N.W., WASHINGTON, D.C.;
F. H. DAVIDSON & CO., 509 W. FRANKLIN ST., BALTIMORE, MD.;
H. A. BERRY, 20 N. SEVENTH STREET, PHILADELPHIA, PA.;
LAZARUS & SMITH, KING & HASELL ST., CHARLESTON, S.C.;
SHURTZ, TOBIN, & CANNON, PORTLAND, ORE.;

And other principal cities in the United States.

For Canada: AIKENHEAD & CROMBIE, King and Yonge Streets, Toronto, Ont.

For Europe and the British Colonies: J. M. RICHARDS, 46 Holborn Viaduct, London, Eng.

AGENTS WANTED.

CHAS. S. PENHALLOW, TREASURER, 505 SEARS BUILDING, BOSTON, MASS.

DAVID R. STRAW, *President.* GEORGE G. PROCTER, *General Manager.*
CHARLES H. FIFIELD, *Treasurer.* J. B. MATHEWS, *Selling Agent.*

MONSON MAINE SLATE COMPANY,

QUARRIERS AND MANUFACTURERS OF

UNFADING BLACK ROOF SLATES,

Urinals, Floor Tiles, Counter Covers, Slabs,

HEADSTONES, GRATE AND REGISTER BORDERS,

Blackboards, Hearthstones, Refrigerator Shelves,

GREENHOUSE TABLES, CHIMNEY TOPS, WASH-TUBS, SINKS, GRAVE VAULTS, LININGS AND COVERS, BASE-BOARDS, WAINSCOTING, WATER-TANKS ELECTRIC SWITCH-BOARDS.

AND SLATE WORK OF EVERY DESCRIPTION.

---

113 DEVONSHIRE STREET,

BOSTON, MASS.

P. O. BOX 2385.

~Whidden & Co~
CONTRACTING
BUILDERS
-101-MILK-ST-BOSTON-
· Water-tight ·
·cellar·work·
·a·specialty·
HEIGHT-252ft
DIAMETER OF
FLUE-13'8"
WEST·END·RLWY·
·CENTRAL·
POWER STATION
Built
in
·1890·

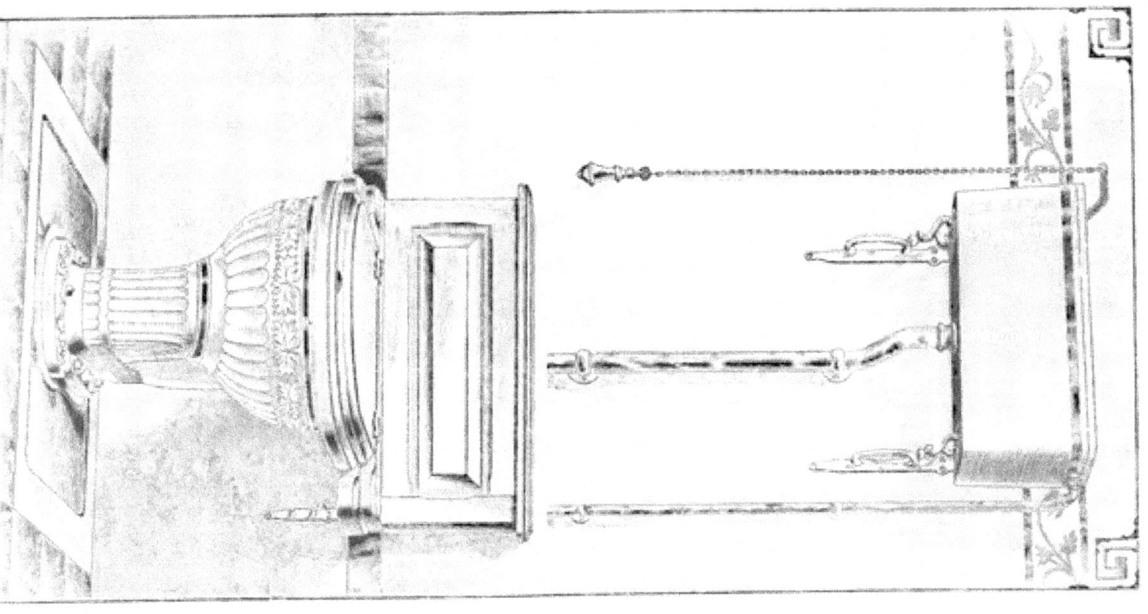

BOSTON SIPHON WATER-CLOSET.

WIRING.

At the present time one of the most important accessories to a new building is the wiring for lighting by electricity. If it is well done in the beginning it is a permanent and satisfactory investment. If poorly done, defects will continually develop, and the entire wiring system become an expensive annoyance. Our work is well done in every case, and all our patrons are our references.

ISOLATED LIGHTING.

The season for making arrangements for the winter's lighting is at hand. If you are considering the introduction of electric lighting in any form, be sure and let us present our apparatus and prices for your consideration. We cannot, in this space, state our claims to your attention; but if you will send us your address we will communicate all the necessary facts to you at once.

FIXTURES.

Nothing among interior decorations adds more to the general attractiveness than the lighting fixtures. At our exhibition-rooms, 25 Otis Street, may be seen the most elegant productions of the designer's skill. We can supply the most fastidious in taste, and in our collection may be found designs suited to any desired expenditure. Do not fail to call on us when selecting this class of goods.

EDISON GENERAL ELECTRIC COMPANY,

25 Otis Street, Boston.

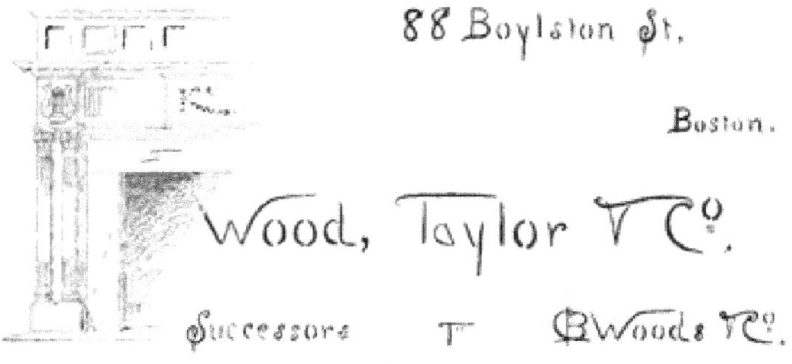
88 Boylston St.
Boston.
Wood, Taylor & Co.
Successors To B Woods & Co.
Manufacturers
of
Wood Mantels, Custom Furniture & Interior Finish.

✦ TILES ✦

HOUSEHOLD ART TILE CO.

88 Boylston St., Boston, Mass.

TILES. :: MOSAICS. :: MARBLE.

ALL KINDS OF FIREPLACE WORK, STAINED AND LEADED GLASS.

SOME BUILDINGS IN BOSTON WE HAVE TILED.

Hotel Vendome, Parker House, Young's Hotel, Adams House, Adams House Café, Hotel Victoria, Hotel Langham, Hotel Reynolds, Hotel Thorndike, Hotel Kensington, Hotel Agassiz, Hotel Grand, Bell Telephone Bldg., Columbia Theatre, Tudor, Ilkley, American House, Hotel Winthrop, Hollman House, Copley, Thompson's Spa, John Hancock Bldg., Hollander & Co., Globe Bldg.

Grand Union Hotel, N. Y. Watson Ins. Bldg., St. Paul, Minn. Building for I. L. G. A. Penn. Co., Philadelphia, Pa.

Refers, by permission, to the Boston Architectural Club.

FAMILY AND OUT OF TOWN ORDERS SOLICITED.

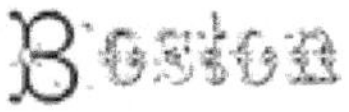

Comp'y

No. 166, ROOM 31, DEVONSHIRE ST., BOSTON, MASS.

Manufacturers of Porous Wares for Floor Arches, Partitions, Furring for Outside Walls and Roofing Tile.

You can save 10 per cent. by using this material to cover your boilers. For further information send for Catalogue.

DAVID McINTOSH, Proprietor.

FACTORY: SCHOOL STREET, REVERE

FRANKLIN SMITH, *President and Treasurer.* ELMER F. SMITH, *Secretary.*

G. W. & F. SMITH IRON CO.

BUILDING IRON WORK.

OFFICE: 411 FEDERAL STREET,

BOSTON.

WROUGHT-IRON WORKS: 409 FEDERAL STREET.

FOUNDRY: FARNHAM STREET BOSTON HIGHLANDS.

Telephone.

F. S. FROST. H. A. LAWRENCE. H. C. GARDNER.

DRAUGHTING INSTRUMENTS

OF EVERY DESCRIPTION.

WHATMAN'S DRAUGHTING PAPERS. ALBERT LEVY'S BLUE-PROCESS PAPERS. TRACING CLOTHS, TRACING PAPERS.

BLUE PRINTING A SPECIALTY.

Architects', Engineers', and Surveyors' Supplies in General. Catalogues furnished on application.

FROST & ADAMS,

IMPORTERS OF ARTISTS' MATERIALS,

37 Cornhill, Boston, Mass.

PAYSON'S

TRANSOM LIFTERS.

The IMPERIAL, UNIVERSAL,

AND

SOLID GRIP.

The **Imperial** *is the finest finish and best working lifter in the market. Only made in Bronze and Brass.*

The **Universal** *and* **Solid Grip** *are made in Bronze, Brass, and Iron.*

Specify them, and

PAYSON'S

PENDULUM PARLOR DOOR-HANGER.

SEND FOR CATALOGUE.

Payson Manufacturing Co., Chicago.

EASTERN OFFICE:

97 CHAMBERS STREET, NEW YORK.

KING'S
WINDSOR
CEMENT
DRY
MORTAR
CO.
OUR DRY MORTAR
IS THE BEST FOR

Plastering Walls and Ceilings.

Our material is 300 per cent. stronger and 200 per cent. harder than lime and hair mortar, and will not rust iron.

Houses in which this plaster is used can be occupied four to six weeks earlier than they could if ordinary mortar were employed.

SEND for our CIRCULARS before plastering your buildings.

King's Windsor Cement Dry Mortar Co.,
166 Devonshire Street, Boston.

New York Office, Times Building.

www.ingramcontent.com/pod-product-compliance
Lightning Source LLC
Chambersburg PA
CBHW030822270326
41928CB00007B/855
* 9 7 8 3 7 4 2 8 3 3 8 9 1 *